NO SEO FOREVER

Focus On Ultimate Traffic
Sources That Are More Reliable,
Stable, and Viral

HARSHAJYOTI DAS

1

2014 by *Harshajyoti Das*

Disclaimer and Terms of Use: The Author and Publisher has strived to be as accurate and complete as possible in the creation of this book, notwithstanding the fact that he does not warrant or represent at any time that the contents within are accurate due to the rapidly changing nature of the Internet. While all attempts have been made to verify information provided in this publication, the Author and Publisher assumes no responsibility for errors, omissions, or contrary interpretation of the subject matter herein. Any perceived slights of specific persons, peoples, or organizations are unintentional. In practical advice books, like anything else in life, there are no guarantees of results. Readers are cautioned to rely on their own judgment about their individual circumstances and act accordingly. This book is not intended for use as a source of legal, medical, business, accounting or financial advice. All readers are advised to seek services of competent professionals in the legal, medical, business, accounting, and finance fields.

First Published, 2014

Dedication

To my wife who inspired me to write and helped
me throughout the editing process

About the Author

Harshajyoti Das

Harsh is the CEO and Co-Founder of Munmi IT Solutions LLP.

He is a traveler, a writer, an inbound marketer (SEO'er), an entrepreneur, and a business adviser.

His first book, "How to write content that converts 600% More" is a bestseller. http://amzn.to/1niszm5

He helps upcoming entrepreneurs by offering them motivational tips and internet marketing advice on his blog, FireYourMentor.com

Table of Contents

7

Introduction

Focus On Ultimate Traffic Sources That Are More Reliable, Stable, and Viral !

I am so tired of Panda and Penguin updates!

Traffic sources that we will discuss in this book:

1. Blogs
2. Forums
3. Q and A Sites
4. Kindle Books
5. Emails
6. Build an 'Asian Sales Army'

Just as a river carries water to the ocean, Google drives traffic to these ultimate traffic sources. Would you rather swim in an ocean or river?

During the last 2 years, Google has rolled out more updates than they have in the previous 10 years. I have personally seen businesses going either bankrupt or suffering severe losses.
Google updates have harmed businesses that solely relied on Google organic traffic more than

those who used PPC advertising, social media, and email marketing.

Some people argue that Google has taken action against black hat SEO. Well, this might be true, but it's not always the case. I held an interview on my blog a couple of days back. One guy who runs an ecommerce store wrote this:

We actually got an outbound links penalty notification in webmaster tools a couple weeks ago, right when the MyBlogGuest penalty happened.

It's hard to find time to write fresh articles when we're constantly adding new product to the site and so many other things, so I posted on MyBlogGuest in 2013 that we would accept a very limited amount of guest posts.

In that whole time, we actually only published seven of the several hundred propels we received. Yeah. Seven posts! These were only good and relevant content, and any outbound links were manually vetted so as not to link to any spammy, irrelevant, or penalized site.

Here's what he said before ending his interview:

The message from Google, though, is clear: guest posting at any kind of scale is going to be treated as harshly as other kinds of link networks. For personal projects, I will continue to use my own careful judgment about guest posting on a case by case basis, but for any kind of client work or for in-house SEO people, guest posting is probably best regarded as a ticking time bomb for your site now.

By the way, if you are wondering - MyBlogGuest is a forum where guest authors can find blogs to write articles. Google penalized any website that gained links or published an article using MyBlogGuest on 20th March, 2014. You can read the whole interview here:
http://fireyourmentor.com/13-experts-share-their-take-on-guest-blogging-after-google-penalised-myblogguest-forums/

So, Google's not just penalizing black hat sites, but anybody who tries to "build a link". You heard it right. You can't build links, you must earn them. Only that's termed as ethical by Google.

By the end of 2013, Google said press releases should 'no follow' all their links. In March 2014, Google stated that all blog posts made by guest authors should be 'no followed'. Google's been cutting down on each and every link building technique known to man.

In a recent interview, a guy asked me, "Where do you see the future of SEO?"

My reply was,

SEO is not dead yet, but will be dead soon. Google's trying to bring everything under their control. Let me explain. Recently, Matt Cutts said that guest posting links should be no followed and shouldn't affect page rank. Well, now name one legit link building method where you are allowed to build links to rank higher or pass page rank (in Matt Cutts's words).

Of course, there are methods like hosting interviews, expert roundups, pointing out broken links to webmasters, designing logos for free in exchange for a link, etc., but they are all going to become invalid soon. It's not far when Google will ask you to 'no follow' these links as well. The shift is already happening. Very soon Google will devalue all the link building practices that cannot be brought under their direct control.

I have seen many micro-niche amazon affiliate sites rank on the first page and make over $100/month in revenue, without a single *backlink. The only promotion that was done was <u>G+ shares</u> (yeah, it was a test!).*

Think about <u>a future</u> where websites will rank on Google based on their influence on Google+. If someone tries to manipulate the system, Google will instantly ban them. SEO'rs will still be in business, but instead of 'link building', they will have to shift to 'G+ share earning' and 'Google Authorship'. So, you will need to start creating content, videos, and images that are shared more often on Google+. In the future, Google might still consider Tweets and Facebook shares as ranking factors, but like I said earlier, they will try to focus on ranking factors that they can control directly.

Let's not forget that Google hides over 80% of search terms on Google Analytics. This means that you will have no idea about keywords that people are searching for to land on your site.

Some people can argue that they will not get any traffic to their site if they do not focus on traffic from Google. It's not really true. There are sources that can send enormous amounts of traffic to your site. I am not talking about running advertisements or PPC ads. I am talking about social media sites, blogs, forums, and Q & A sites that are more viral.

I opened my blog, FireYourMentor.com, in late Oct. 2013. The site has less content because I have had much less time to earn links. I will not build any black hat links, but will wait for the links to come in naturally. But meanwhile, I need traffic, and the only way left for me is to earn it via alternate sources, I will discuss that in this book.

Here's a screenshot of my traffic from Google Analytics. I was getting just over 20 visitors every day to my site.

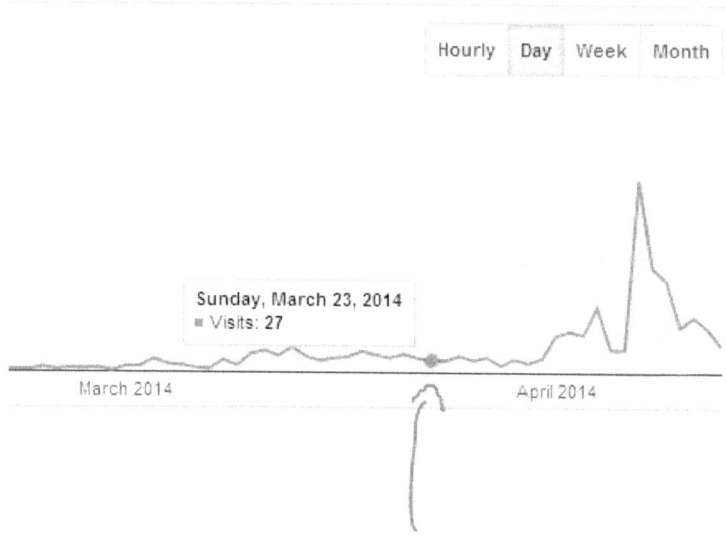

After I did some promotions on social media sites, 3rd party blogs, content curation sites, and forums, I was able to increase my traffic by a huge margin in April.

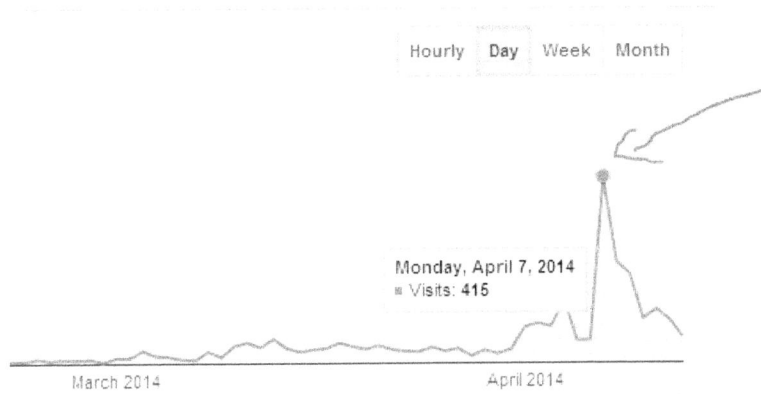

I received <u>over 450 social shares</u> for the blog post that went viral on 7th April.

11 Experts Talk About Building a Brand on Social Media Sites

As I am writing this book, today is the 14th of April. Let me show you the last seven days traffic stats.

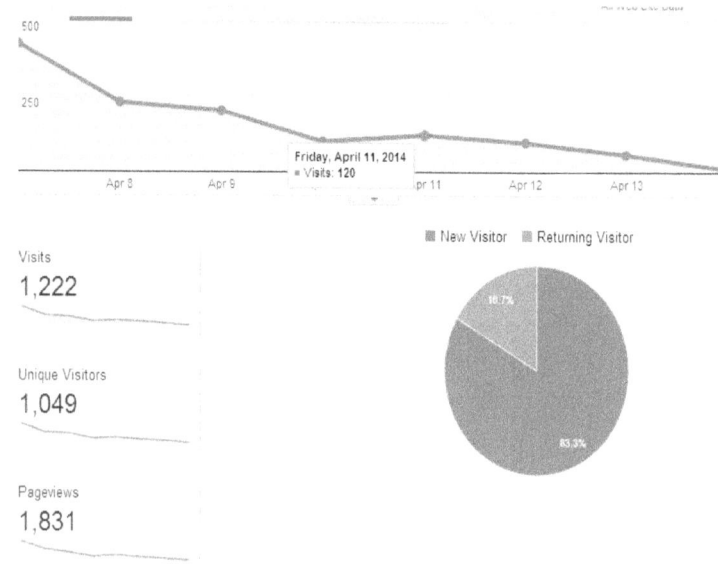

I am getting around 100 visitors every day. Let's take, for example, 12th April. I have received 96 visitors, and just 4 were from Google. The rest were either direct referral or from social media sites.

Here, take a look:

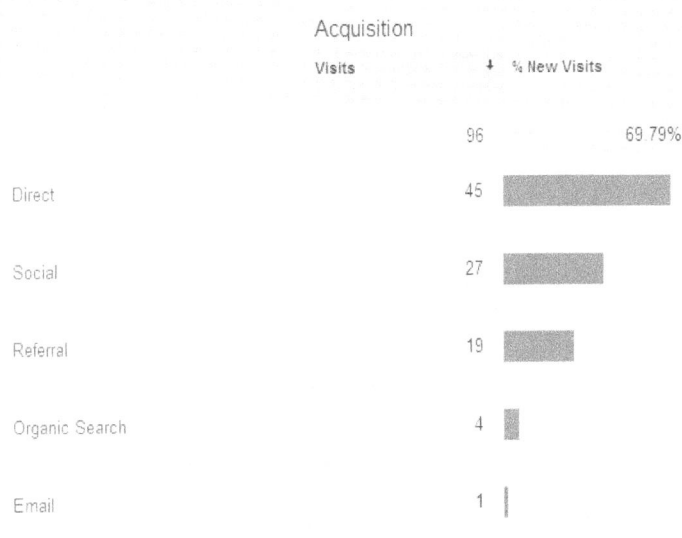

Remember when I said in my interview earlier that social shares will play an important role in determining Google ranking? **Here's proof.**

When you search for my name, the article with 450+ social shares on FireYourMentor.com shows up on the first page. This article has no links built. It's interesting to see that Google has decided to show this particular article instead of showing the homepage or any other article.

Backlinks still play a role, but Google's heading towards making social shares one of the major ranking factors. The future I talked about earlier is not too far away.

I will give you one more reason to quit doing SEO. Most people build multiple 'niche websites' and want to create a stream of passive income. What they don't know is that Google is more likely to rank an authority site above their small niche website.

If you create niche websites, you will have to run after rankings. If you run after rankings, it means you can't do white hat SEO. People who do white hat SEO don't run after rankings. You will have to opt for blackhat SEO. Now, here's the issue. Google's been cracking down on sites that are built to rank. If your idea is to create multiple niche websites and create a passive income stream, it's not going to happen. You are only creating some churn & burn sites that will be taken down by Google after 2-3 months. What will you do after that? Are you going to play this temporary game for your whole life?

Perhaps a better idea would be to create a "Niche Authority" site. You can expand when the first one is successful. Build it like a company. It should be the ultimate resource in your niche.

Think of an activity you love doing. If you don't love it, you will lose interest. Once you find your niche, become an authority around that niche. When you have one authority site to focus on, you don't need to rely on Google. You can easily earn 100+ visitors daily with social media and referral traffic alone.

Like I said, earlier, build it like a company. Network with others on social media sites. They will help you drive traffic and promo your content. That's the beginning. Once you have a lot of content on your site, long tail keywords will automatically start ranking on Google. So forget about SEO. Focus on traffic instead.

Now that you have my attention, let's start talking about the various alternate sources that will make you say, "No SEO Forever!"

Chapter 1

BLOGS

Things we will cover in this chapter:

1. What Is Guest Posting?
2. How To Find Blogs To Guest Post On?
3. How Do You Know How Much Traffic You Will Get From These Blog Posts?
4. Why Should You Do Guest Posting For Traffic And Not For Links?
5. The Power Of Blog Commenting
6. Finding Targeted Blogs With Commentluv Plugin Installed
7. Why Should You Have A Blog, And How Do You Gain Traffic?
8. How To Gain Hundreds Of Social Shares Within A Day?
9. How To Make A Blog Go Viral ?
10. How To Find Content And Automate For Your Blog?

What Is Guest Posting?

When someone writes an article for someone else's website as a guest author, he either does it to drive traffic to his site or to interact with the audience of that blog.

Guest posting is an opportunity that's rare because not everyone can do justice with their writing on someone else's blog. Most guest posting opportunities come with personal connections.

However, there are blogs that accept guest posts from any good writer. We will discuss in detail how you can find those prospective blogs to accept your article.

Initially, the concept of guest blogging was similar to writing for a magazine. Eventually, people started writing not for the audience but to gain backlinks. That's when Google stepped in and said that if you want to post a backlink on your guest post, that's fine, but it should be 'no followed'.

Guest posting should be done with the sole intention of reaching an audience, to demonstrate your knowledge and authority on a particular topic. People will start following you on Twitter and Facebook once they recognize you as the 'leader' in your industry.

How To Find Blogs To Guest Post On?

I have found an effective way of finding highly targeted blogs. I scan a guy in my industry who does regular guest blogging. Then, I search his/her posts in Google.

Ann Smarty, founder of MyBlogGuest and Viral Content Buzz, is a well-known blogger in the SEO industry.

Let's say I want to track guest posts made by Ann Smarty. I would:

Go to Google and search for *"Ann Smarty" inurl:/author/*

Google   "Ann Smarty" inurl:/author/

Web   Images   Shopping   Videos   News   More ▾   Search tools

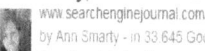

About 1,760 results (0.38 seconds)

Ann Smarty, Author at Search Engine Journal

www.searchenginejournal.com/**author/ann-smarty**/ ▾
by Ann Smarty - in 33,645 Google+ circles
Ann Smarty is the blogger and community manager at Internet Marketing
Ninjas. Ann's expertise in blogging and tools serve as a base for her writing,
tutorials ...

1) PA: 71   1,416 Links / PRO ONLY RDs   **DA: 85**   PRO ONLY Links / PRO ONLY RDs   ⊘ Link Analysis

Ann Smarty - Community/Branding Manager and Internet ...

www.internetmarketingninjas.com/blog/**author/ann-smarty**/ ▾
by Ann Smarty - in 33,645 Google+ circles
As Community and Brand manager, **Ann Smarty's** work is focused on both regularly
contributing to the Internet Marketing Ninjas blog and serving as an internal ...

2) PA: 64   2,547 Links / PRO ONLY RDs   **DA: 71**   PRO ONLY Links / PRO ONLY RDs   ⊘ Link Analysis

Ann Smarty, Author at - Social Media Examiner

www.socialmediaexaminer.com/**author/ann-smarty**/ ▾
by Ann Smarty - in 33,645 Google+ circles
May 8, 2012 - social media how to Hosting a Twitter chat is an amazing way to interact
with your fans and followers. to better understand and grow your ...

3) PA: 49   43 Links / PRO ONLY RDs   **DA: 85**   PRO ONLY Links / PRO ONLY RDs   ⊘ Link Analysis

Ann Smarty, Author at The Daily Egg | The Daily Egg

blog.crazyegg.com/**author/ann-smarty**/ ▾
About **Ann Smarty**. **Ann Smarty** is the founder of MyBlogGuest, co-founder of
ViralContentBuzz and Brand manager at Internet Marketing Ninjas. Ann is an active ...

4) PA: 35   1 Links / PRO ONLY RDs   **DA: 79**   PRO ONLY Links / PRO ONLY RDs   ⊘ Link Analysis

You   can   also   use   this   footprint:

[inpostauthor:"*ann smarty*"]

Alternatively, you can also search for the exact author's bio and paste it in Google. Google will return results for all the blogs where the author's bio was found.

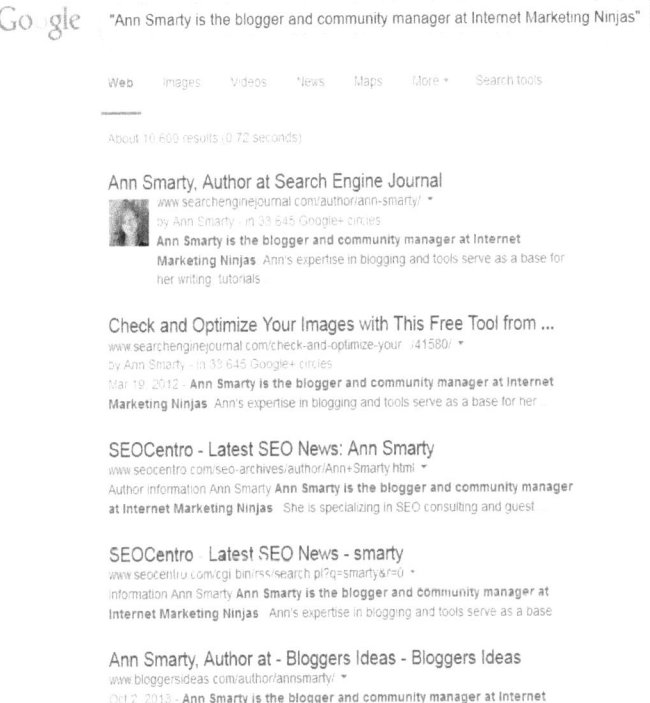

You can select any influencer in your niche and find all the guest posts he/she has made. Once you have a good list of blogs that accept blog posts from authors, you can pitch them your article ideas.

There are a couple of ways to find blogs that accept guest posts. The most popular technique is by searching for a few footprints in Google.

1. "Submit Guest Post"
2. "submit guest post"
3. "Group Writing Project"
4. inurl:guest-posts
5. "Guest Contributor"
6. "Send your post"
7. inurl:guest-post-guidelines
8. "want to write for"
9. keyword "write for us"
10. keyword "guest post guidelines"
11. "Become a Contributor"
12. "Guest Bloggers Wanted"
13. keyword + submit an article
14. "Bloggers Wanted"
15. "the following guest post"
16. "Become a Guest Writer"
17. "Suggest a guest post"
18. keyword + write for us
19. "blogs accepting guest posts"
20. "Submission Guidelines"
21. "The following guest post"
22. keyword "guest post"

23. keyword "guest posting"
24. "guest posts roundup"
25. "my guest posts"
26. keyword "accepting guest posts"
27. "Submit a guest post" / "Submit post" / "Submit blog post"
28. "Submit [keyword] News"
29. "become a guest blogger"
30. "Guest post by"
31. "Submit News"
32. "write for us"
33. "Add blog post"
34. "Now Accepting Guest Posts"
35. inurl:write-for-us
36. "Contribute to our Site"
37. "Become an Author"
38. "group writing project"
39. "Contribute"
40. inurl:guest-posts
41. "submit a guest post"
42. "Submit Blog Post"
43. "contribute"
44. "guest post guidelines"
45. "Add Guest Post"
46. "Publish Your News"
47. "guest post"
48. [keyword] + contribute
49. [Keyword] + guest blogging

50. [Keyword] "guest blogging"
51. [Keyword] "submit an article"
52. "now accepting guest posts"
53. "this guest post is from"
54. "add guest post"
55. "Blogs Accepting Guest Posts"
56. "Submit a Guest Article"
57. "Submit an article"
58. "Suggest a Guest Post"
59. keyword + submit your post
60. "blogs that accept guest posts"
61. "suggest a guest post"
62. "this guest post was written"
63. "bloggers wanted"
64. "Guest Posts Roundup"
65. "Submit Tutorial"
66. "Guest Post Guidelines"
67. "This is a guest article"
68. "Submit a Guest Post"
69. "Become a Guest Blogger"
70. "This guest post was written"
71. "become a contributor"
72. "guest blogging spot"
73. "this is a guest post by"
74. "Suggest a Post"
75. "Send a guest post"
76. "guest post by"
77. "Guest Bloggers Wanted"

78. "contribute to our site"
79. inurl:write-for-us
80. keyword + submit post
81. "Write for Us"
82. "Community News"
83. inurl:guest-post-guidelines
84. keyword "submit post"
85. "this is a guest article"
86. "guest contributor"
87. "Blogs that Accept Guest Posts"
88. keyword "submit a guest post"
89. keyword + submit guest post
90. "Blogs that Accept Guest Bloggers"
91. "guest bloggers wanted"
92. "Become a Contributor"
93. inurlprofiles/blog/new
94. "Blogs that Accept Guest Blogging"
95. "Places I Guest Posted"
96. "become a guest writer"
97. "Add Articlcs"
98. "submission guidelines"
99. "places i guest posted"
100.   "Want to Write for"
101.   "My Guest Posts"
102.   "submit a guest article"
103.   "This guest post is from"
104.   "become an author"
105.   keyword "guest post by"

106.   "blogs that accept guest bloggers"
107.   "Guest Post"
108.   "Guest Blogging Spot"

Instead of searching for footprints in Google, you can also search for blogs in various blog directories, content curation sites and contact them individually.

Here's a list of blog directories and platforms from where you can find blogs and contact them.

- http://guestblogit.com/
- http://blogs.botw.org/
- http://www.ontoplist.com/blog-directory/
- http://bloggerlinkup.com/
- http://guestr.com/
- http://www.blogdash.com/
- http://www.postjoint.com/
- http://www.copyforbylines.com/
- http://guestbloggingwebsites.com/
- http://www.blogsynergy.com/
- https://www.guestbloggenius.com/
- http://alltop.com/
- http://blogsearch.google.com/
- http://www.fizzniche.com/
- http://technorati.com/blogs/directory/
- http://blogs.botw.org/

- http://mykbt.com/bloggeries
- http://portal.eatonweb.com/
- http://www.ontoplist.com/
- http://www.blogged.com/
- http://www.blogsearchengine.com/
- http://www.blogcatalog.com/
- http://www.globeofblogs.com/
- http://www.britblog.com/
- http://www.biggerblogger.com/
- http://www.blogflux.com/
- http://www.bloglisting.net/
- http://www.blogdigger.com/index.html

Another interesting way to get guest blogging opportunities is by asking your website subscribers, YouTube subscribers, Twitter followers, and Facebook friends, if they would invite you to write a guest post on their blog.

How Do You Know How Much Traffic You Will Get From These Blog Posts?

The last thing you want to do is spend your precious time writing for a blog that receives no traffic and has no audience.
You need to find blogs that have traffic and visibility.

I like to keep a spreadsheet like this:

	B	C	D	E	F	G	H
1	**Website Details**			**Website Engagement**			
2	Website URL	PR	DA	Avg Comments	Avg Fb shares	Avg Tweets	Avg G+
3	www.searchenginejournal.com	6	86	3	150	300	50
4	http://moz.com/ugc	na	93	20	30	90	10
5	http://www.searchenginepeople.c	5	66	2	10	35	10
6	http://dailyseotip.com	4	48	3	5	30	5
7	http://www.hobo-web.co.uk/seo-t	4	59	na	7	15	7
8	http://seo2.0.onreact.com	na	55	5	na	na	10
9	http://www.toprankblog.com	6	81	5	80	400	40
10	http://www.socialmediaexaminer.	6	86	20	700	1000	100
11	http://bloggless.com	0	30	30	70	121	88
12	http://www.aliensmoney.com	0	31	10	50	30	3
13	http://www.techivy.com/	2	25	10	10	50	3
14	cdnify.com	2	35	2			
15	http://berichandrich.com/	0	13	4	12	2	1
16	http://www.bloggersideas.com/	0	31	4	10	15	10

Here's a list of all the metrics that you need to verify before shortlisting a blog to write a guest post on:

1. Alexa Rank
2. Page Rank
3. Domain Authority
4. Page Authority
5. Avg. Comments
6. Avg. Facebook shares
7. Avg. Tweets
8. Avg. G+

If you have noticed, I haven't created a column for Alexa Rankings in my spreadsheet. That's because I check the Alexa Rankings of each blog even before pasting them on to the spreadsheet.

Usually, I try to shortlist blogs that have an Alexa ranking of less than 500K. Alexa Rankings don't mean much if the other metrics are good.

In case you don't know how to check for these metrics, I recommend using a free plugin for Firefox and Chrome. It's called SEOQUAKE.

Why Should You Do Guest Posting For Traffic And Not For Links?

Google has recently penalized a popular forum called MyBlogGuest for promoting guest blogging. It's funny, because they were not a blog network. There were legit blog owners who used their site to get interested guest authors to write articles for them.

Matt Cutts, head of the Google Search team, said that all guest posting links should be 'no followed'. It was a clear indication that Google doesn't want you to guest post just for the sake of SEO or getting your site ranked on Google.

In the near future, you can expect Google to take more strict actions on websites that try to gain links using guest blogging.

The Question Is, Can Guest Blogging Really Send Traffic To Your Site?

Well, yes. If you write a great piece of content in a popular blog or a magazine, readers will be curious to know who you are. They will search for your work, subscribe to your blog feeds, and follow you on Twitter and other social media sites.

Guest blogging doesn't work for those who write substandard articles because they are posting it on somebody else's site. It backfires. You will not only waste your time writing that article, but also prove that you do not have adequate knowledge on that topic.

People who love automation and outsourcing can even get it written by a content writer. Just supervise his/her work and infuse your knowledge inside the article. It will save you time.

Firstly, they will rank well on Google as you will post them on high authority websites. Secondly, these articles will attract a lot of links and social shares (as these blogs will already have an audience).

Even after a year or two, they will continue ranking on Google and on other (future) search engines. So, it's not just a one year investment - you are making a long term investment.

Let's Do Some Simple Math.

Let's say you have posted 100 articles within a span of one year on various blogs and magazines. Each article is well researched, and you target 4-5 keywords within it (via h1, h2, h3 tags).

If an article ranks for 4-5 long tail keywords that have a combined monthly search of at least 500 visitors, each article will receive around 6000 visitors in a year. It amounts to **600,000 visitors for all your 100 articles**. Even if 5% of people visit your site via the referral links, you will receive 36,000 visitors within a year. That's **3,000 visitors every month** or **100 visitors daily**.

Of course, this assumption will depend on a variety of factors like keyword research, their ability to rank, link placement, author's bio, copywriting skills, etc. But you get the idea, right?

The Power of Blog Commenting

Blog commenting is very powerful, especially when you place high quality comments on relevant websites. I am not talking only from a SEO perspective. It does help with SEO, but you should focus on getting all that referral traffic to your site.

It's wise to sneak in a link in these comments. If that's not possible, it's alright. WordPress allows commenters to post a link back to their site by hyperlinking the name.

Here are some advantages of blog commenting:

1. Since most of the comments are no follow, they won't provide any real SEO benefits, but 'do follow' links will.
2. Blog commenting will help you increase your domain and page authority. Evidently, authority does pass, even if a link has 'no follow' tags.
3. Referral traffic, which is highly laser targeted to your niche/topic.
4. Branding. If you use your 'name'+ 'gravatar', to post comments, it will help with your personal branding. When a person searching for a particular topic finds you in each and every article he reads, you will definitely catch his

attention. He will be like, "Who is this guy who comments on this topic so often? He must have a lot of knowledge about this topic. Let me find more about him."

5. Reputation Management on Google. Many People don't know that their comments get indexed on Google. Now, whenever someone searches for your "name" on Google, they will immediately get a glimpse of all the blogs where you have left a comment. It will show that you are an expert in your field. It will also keep negative press at bay.

6. You get to learn more about a particular topic when you go through all these articles. You are ultimately enhancing your knowledge.

How To Build Relationships With Blog Commenting?

Blog commenting can also be used to build relationships by replying to comments. If you make it a habit of reading the comments and replying to them, people will eventually start noticing you. People who leave a comment behind love to get a reply from others.

If you are active on popular blogs in your niche or industry, and interact regularly with others, you will build a healthy relationship. It's networking in the cloud. Talk to them, appreciate their views, and add your own views.

If you make a habit of networking 30 minutes daily on popular blogs and forums, you will eventually become an authority and an influencer. It's not the goal you should worry about. Focus on the process, the process of replying to comments every day.

Finding Targeted Blogs With Commentluv & Keyword Luv Plugin Installed

Commentluv is a plugin for WordPress introduced by Andy Baily. It enables a blog owner to change the links from 'no follow' to 'do follow' in comments.

Commentluv gives users an option to link back to one of their latest posts from within the comment. It also enables commenters to leave their Twitter ID while commenting. Blog owners use Commentluv plugin to encourage people to comment on their blogs.

Keywordluv plugin, on the other hand, has a feature to hyperlink a keyword while commenting. Thus, it helps you to get a do follow link back to your site with your targeted anchor text.

Anyways, we are not here to talk about link building. You can use blogs that use Commentluv and Keywordluv to drive targeted referral traffic to your blog post on a similar topic.

There are not many blogs that use these plugins, but you will be able to find a few in your niche if you do a Google search with some specific footprints.

Footprint to find blogs that use the CommentLuv Premium Plugin

"Your Keyword" *"This blog uses Premium CommentLuv"*

Footprint to find blogs that use the CommentLuv Premium Plugin

"Your Keyword" *"Enter Your name@Your Keywords"*

Tell you what? I will save you the trouble of copy and pasting the footprints on Google. You can use either http://www.putmylink.com/ or http://dropmylink.com/ to automate it.

I use a software called 'scrapebox' to scrape blogs that have a CommentLuv & KeywordLuv plugin installed.

A Universal Comment for Every Blog

When you are short of time, you can use a universal comment that will be accepted on any blog you comment on. Obviously, you can come up with your own version but here's mine:

That's a lot of information. I have been reading this blog for quite some time. Every time I come back to visit, I find another great article to read. Thanks, keep up the good work.

You can customize the same reply for different blogs by adding a sentence about the blog topic. Here's how I like to do it:

I have always been a fan and I'm always interested to learn more about [blog topic]. That's a lot of information to consume on [blog topic]. I have been reading this blog for quite some time. Every time I come back to visit, I find another great article to read. Thanks, keep up the good work.

If you have written a similar article on your blog, then feel free to link that article like this:

I have always been a fan and I'm always interested to learn more about [blog topic]. That's a lot of information to consume on [blog topic]. I have been reading this blog for quite some time. Every time I come back to visit, I find another great article to read. Thanks, keep up the good work.

I have written a similar article on [blog topic]. http://article-link.com

Is it fine if I quote you in my article?

The acceptance ratio usually decreases when you post a link along with your comment, but it's definitely worth a shot, as you will increase your referral traffic by more than 10 times. Do some split tests and keep a record. Compare the acceptance ratio.

You can check off "Notify me about follow up comments via e-mail". In most cases, the blog owner will reply to your comment and thank you. It's a nice way of keeping a track of how many comments get accepted. Use a separate email for commenting. That way the email won't get spammed. It's always better to avoid free email service providers like Gmail or Yahoo. Instead, use your own domain with SMTP.

Here's a tip to get more comments accepted:

1. Use a Gravatar (https://www.gravatar.com/)
2. Always use your real name (good for online reputation management)

Why Should You Have A Blog, and How Do You Gain Traffic?

You may have a website, but you also need a blog to drive targeted traffic to your site.

Let me explain with the help of an example.

Let's say Mr. Joseph has a website, via which he sells a few skin care and anti-aging products. If he opens up a blog to help people, he can grow his subscriber base. Ultimately, he can divert that traffic from his blog to his sales page. Even if he sells anti-aging product, he can have articles related to health and wellness, personal development, or even retirement planning (since his target audience is around 40-60). Once his audience knows that Mr. Joseph provides real value, they will trust him better. According to behavioral psychology, it's easier to persuade a customer if he knows you personally and trusts your work.

A blog provides a platform to build relationships by solving people's problems. If a business owner doesn't have the time to write blog posts, he can very well hire a content developer to take care of its content marketing needs.

There are a few things you need to remember while writing a blog post:

1. Write big fat articles - usually above 2,000 words. You need to provide an ultimate guide for your readers.
2. Do your keyword research before writing a blog post. If you target low competitive long tail keywords, your blog has a possibility of ranking easily on Google without the need for any SEO.
3. Write link bait titles to increase the click through rates and social sharing.
4. Make your blog post visually appealing (with images and videos).

5. Make sure you have the keyword in your title and URL.

You needn't think about building links or doing any SEO for your blog. Keep on writing content. Once you have 50+ articles, you will see that people will start to link back automatically, and your blog will eventually rank on Google.

Link-bait titles means:

It's a term that usually refers to a 'Title' that's solely written to get more links and shares.

Here's an example:

A Normal article title:

❖ "A guide on dog training"

Link bait article title:

❖ "The craziest guide to train your dog in 10 minutes a day"
❖ "7 things you never knew about training your dog"
❖ "Scooby Blackbook - Train your dog to be the next Scooby"

How to Gain Hundreds of Social Shares within A Day?

In order to gain traffic to your blog right from Day 1, I use a platform called ViralContentBuzz.com. It helps you to gain a lot of social signals within a few hours.

After the initial boost, it can even go viral on all social media sites if you have a high-quality article.

Here's how Viralcontentbuzz.com works?

When you share content of other people related to your niche, you earn credits.

You can use the same credits to list your article, and other people will share it so that they can gain more credits.

How is it different from other social exchange platforms?

Well, it's moderated. They do not allow low quality blogs, or blogs that have a sales pitch or an affiliate program.

I usually spend around 150-200 credits per article.

Once, an article went viral on StumbleUpon, and I received over 200+ visitors along with 100+ stumbles on my article. Another day, I received over 100 pins on Pinterest.

There's another method, you can use. Host interviews and expert roundups! You can find your prospects from websites like HARO (http://www.helpareporter.com). People are fanatic about getting press and popularity. You can leverage the same eagerness to get some social signals on your site.

When you interview an expert on your blog, he is all excited to tell the whole world about it. Hence, he will share it on social media sites, email his subscribers, or even add a link on his blog under 'press coverage'.

I managed to get hundreds of social signals when I did an expert round-up a few days back.

This expert round-up received **486 social shares.**

http://fireyourmentor.com/11-experts-talk-about-building-a-brand-on-social-media-sites/

Another expert round-up received **251 social shares.**

http://fireyourmentor.com/36-entrepreneurs-share-their-secrets-on-how-to-generate-an-idea-special-thanks-to-james-altucher/

When you have 10-20 experts, each one of them will share it with their audience. Thus, your blog will get a lot of visibility, along with social shares by their respective fans and followers.

Let me share with you the exact email template I send to interviewees after I publish their interview.

Hello XYZ,
Your interview was published here: http://link-to-the-article.com

Please see if it's all good. If something needs to be edited, let me know.

I will highly appreciate if you could share it with your friends and followers. Kindly upvote it on [Inbound.org/hacker news/kinged] as well: http://link-to-a-content-curation-site.com

1-click share links *[created it with hrefshare.com]:* Facebook | Twitter | Google+ | Linkedin

Thank You.

Regards,
My Name

Designation

Company: *(website)*
Email: *my@email.com*
Twitter: *https://twitter.com/my-profile*
Facebook: *https://www.facebook.com/my-profile*
Google Plus: *https://plus.google.com/my-profile*
LinkedIn: *http://www.linkedin.com/pub/my-profile*

How to Make a Blog Go Viral?

What are the essential qualities for a blog to go viral on the internet? If you don't make an effort with marketing during the initial phase, it won't get any visibility.

Like I said earlier, you have to make a certain amount of effort to get the first 50-100 shares. Gain some 'social proof'. Once that's done, people will get to see your articles on social media sites. If it's of very high quality, people will obviously share it.

You will need to take care of a few things though:

- The content should be visually appealing
- Write Link bait 'titles'
- Use jaw-dropping images if you are promoting it on Pinterest and StumbleUpon.
- Use #hashtag on Twitter, Facebook and Google+

You will also need to submit it on content curation sites. In my niche, I submit it to inbound.org, Hacker News, and kingged.com. It is better to find content curation sites in your respective niche.

How to Find Content and Automate For Your Blog?

There are a few ways to get content and automate the whole content writing and posting process.

1. Hire article writers from Fiverr.com, odesk.com or elance.com
2. Hold expert roundups

3. Hold individual interviews (special authors)
4. Accept guest bloggers on your website

You will be able to hire a content writer to write 500 words for $5 on Fiverr. Make sure you give him the necessary details and instructions. Most writers would just re-write content from the internet. If you want originality, tell your writer beforehand.

You can hold expert roundups by posting queries on HARO (http://www.helpareporter.com).

To hold individual interviews, I usually find best-selling authors in my niche (on Amazon) and contact people via Facebook. It's easy to find authors and influencers by searching their names. You can also contact them via the contact form on their website, LinkedIn or Twitter. Let's not forget that you can of course use HARO for individual interviews as well.

When you accept guest bloggers, it might be tough to get guest articles, especially when your blog is new, without any page rank or traffic. Still, it's better to accept guest authors right from the beginning. That way, you will get a few pitches every now and then.

On my blog, FireYourMentor.com, I have a page for guest authors where the instructions are mentioned in great detail.

Say, for example, I don't accept guest articles that are less than 2000 words. The authors understand exactly what kind of articles get published on the blog. Thus, you can avoid hundreds of sub-standard guest blogging requests by link builders.

Clearly mention the following instructions _(you can add more if you want)_:

1. Minimum words of an article
2. Minimum number of images along with the article
3. Topics, article ideas
4. Only stock images or images that the writer owns can be used
5. Examples of other articles the writer has written
6. Social profiles of the writer
7. How should a writer send you the article for approval

And the list goes on...

Chapter 2

Forums

Things we will cover in this chapter:

1. How to attract traffic from forums?
2. How to become an influencer in your niche?
3. Which forums to target?
4. Buying signature links on these forums
5. Buying banners on these forums
6. Hiring a VA for this job

How to Attract Traffic from Forums?

Are you active on any forum related to your niche? If not, then find a forum and sign up for it. You can then come back and continue reading this book.

Most forums will have an option to put your 'signature link' in your posts. Some forums will require their members to post a few replies before enabling this feature.

You can use these signature links to send traffic from these forums to your site or a landing page. Linking your signature directly to your website is not a very smart idea. It will of course help you to deliver referral traffic to your site, but what you need is an audience and loyal followers.

Try to grab their emails by offering a small report or a freebie. If you have an ecommerce site, give away coupons in exchange for an email. If you have a blog, give away a free eBook or free software. The possibilities are endless.

When I was promoting my first book, "How to Write Content That Converts 600% More", I linked them to a landing page (designed with unbounce.com). I asked for their email addresses and told them that I would notify them on the launch day. They will get my book for a special launch price of 99 cents. A reader who is really eager to read the book will obviously sign up for it. It was a win-win scenario.

What type of reports should you create? How do you create them?

A 250 page book sells for $4-5 on Kindle, whereas a 15 page eBook sells for $7 on Warrior Forum (as a WFO product). It's because warrior members consider every purchase as an investment. If they can earn more than $10 after reading this WFO, it's a winner. On the other hand, people look for a better reading experience on Kindle. We see people posting negative reviews about grammatical errors, lack of graphics, excessive use of graphs, and a ton of other things.

I have given you a comparison between a Kindle book and a WFO eBook so that you know that you don't need to focus on the number of pages if you target the right audience. People will be happy to receive a free report of 5 pages in exchange for their email ID. It does not need to be 50 pages long.

You can create a free report on any major news, statistical facts about an industry, or a personalized evaluation. If you are in the web design industry, you can offer a free website evaluation report. If you are in the health industry, you can offer free diet plans for a specific disease.

Creating a report is as easy as it can get. You can either create a PowerPoint presentation and convert it into a video or write a Word document and convert it into a PDF.

How to Become an Influencer in Your Niche?

Whenever a query pops up, reply as soon as you can. Firstly, if you are the first to reply, your answer will stay on top within the thread.

Secondly, it will get a lot more visibility. Thirdly, you can expect to get a quick reply from the guy who answered your query. He might even start following you on Twitter because the next time he has a doubt, he knows whom to call. He can simply mention you on Twitter (using @) and ask a query. That's how new relationships are built.

Write Ultimate Guides

Have you ever come across 1000-3000 word threads? These are called the Ultimate guides. Influencers often practice this technique to establish themselves as an authority on a forum or a discussion board.

These guides are just like a how-to article, but instead they are more elaborate, detailed, and 'original'. It's usually a concept or an idea that an influencer comes up with on his own, and then he shares it with the forum members. If it's an original idea, people will instantly recognize it.

That gives him credibility and authority. The next time he posts something or sells something, people will trust him.

How do you gain that knowledge?

Read books, watch YouTube videos, talk with influencers, interview experts. There are 'n' numbers of ways to gain enough knowledge on a particular topic.

Recently, I had an interest in learning behavior psychology. So, I signed up for a course on Alison.com (http://alison.com/courses/Diploma-in-Psychology). Then, I went to Amazon.com and brought 3 books (Influence, Predictably Irrational, and What Every BODY is Saying). Finally, I went on YouTube and watched all the videos posted by Derek Halpern on his channel, "Social Triggers". I believe, I will have at least some knowledge to write a 1000 words article on an original idea after learning from these 3 sources.

Which Forums to Target?

You will find tons of forums on the internet, but don't waste your time posting on forums that hardly receive any traffic.

You needn't be active on 20 different forums. Just be active on 3-4 forums that have a lot of traffic.

How do you determine that a forum has traffic?

1. Alexa Rank (aim for forums below 10k)
2. Number of new threads every day
3. Number of new replies every day
4. Number of new members every day

Whenever I need to find a new forum, I look at these four factors. If a forum qualifies on all these four factors, I give it a test run. I post regularly for around a week or two. Once I have my signature link with the help of bit.ly or any other similar service that can track the number of clicks, I can make my decision on the 'quality + quantity' of referral traffic it can send.

Metrics to check for the quality of referral traffic (using Google Analytics on the site):

- Time on site
- Number of page views
- Bounce rate
- Number of goals completed

If I find a certain forum that can send me quality traffic, I continue posting there. If not, I don't waste my time on it.

There are hundreds of footprints for various forum platforms, but the best way is to just Google for the search term: *"keyword forum."*

Also, try to find forums where new members ask more queries than old or established members. It's a sign that the forum is growing.

Buying Signature Links on These Forums

Most people don't know that they can buy signature links on these forums from other members. It's highly lucrative, as it doesn't cost you a fortune.

I have seen people with over 2000 posts renting out their signature space for as low as $5/month. Although the price will vary on different forums, it shouldn't be more than $50/month. You can either get a text link or a banner ad.

How to contact these people?

Sign up and send a private message to them via the forum. They are most likely to respond if they are not using their signature link. Do mention your price. Tell them that you are open to negotiations. It gives them an idea of how much you are planning to spend.

You can also use certain footprints on Google to find these people. Here's one such footprint:

"signature for rent" "keyword"

Buying Banners on These Forums

You can buy banners on most forums. It's cheaper than advertising on a blog or PPC ads. Try contacting the admins of each forum for more information.

Hiring a VA for this job:

I have discussed about hiring a VA in the next chapter as well as in the last chapter, "Asian Sales Army". Please refer accordingly.

Chapter 3

Q and A Sites

Things we will cover in this chapter:

1. What is a Q & A site?
2. What are the popular Q and A sites?
3. Different levels of yahoo answers
4. How to monitor new questions on these sites (use BuzzBundle)
5. Footprints to find more Q and A sites
6. Hiring a dedicated VA for this this job

What Is A Q & A Site?

A Q & A site is a community where people ask questions and another group of people help them by answering. Quora is a classic example of such a website.

The best thing about them is these websites have a lot of long tail traffic. Since, these websites generate thousands of queries everyday, they can rank pretty well on search engines. Hence, it gets a huge chunk of traffic from long tail keywords.

People come to these sites looking for a solutions to their problems. A solution is all they care about.

There are thousands of people with new problems every day in their life. Most of them don't have any loyal friends whom they can trust and share their problems with. Eventually, they post their problem online, and an unknown crowd will start answering them within minutes. Internet has indeed helped us to simplify our lives.

What Are The Popular Q And A Sites?

The most popular ones are 'Quora', 'Yahoo Answers', 'ask.com', 'stackcxchange.com', etc.

If you are active on these four sites, you needn't worry about posting on 20 other sites. Remember, it's useless to focus on sites that have less traffic. Instead, focus on those that have a lot of traffic.

Here's the Alexa Rank of these sites:

• Quora: **435**

- Yahoo Answers: **4**
- ask.com: **30**
- stackexchange.com: **195**

Yahoo Answers:

Yahoo is by far the most widely used Q and A site. Here's an example on how you can reply to a query with a link back to your website. Links are no followed, so they don't help much with your SEO. It will help you big time by sending referral traffic to your site.

It should also be noted that if your answer is selected as the best answer, you will get more visibility than other answers. So instead of just writing a one liner with a link back to your site, write an informative answer that's directed towards solving their problem.

Different Levels of Yahoo Answers

To encourage people to answer, Yahoo has implemented a point & level system. You cannot use these points to redeem or buy anything. You can reach the next level based on the number of points you collect. People usually trust the answer of a level 7 user more than a level 3 user. The chance of being chosen as the best answer also increases, thus increasing your visibility and marketing efforts.

Points and Levels

Action	Points
Begin participating on Yahoo Answers	One Time: 100
Ask a question	-5
Choose a best answer for your question	3
Answer a question	2
Self-deleting an answer	-2
Log in to Yahoo Answers	Once daily: 1
Have your answer selected as the best answer	10
Receive a "thumbs-up" rating on a best answer that you wrote (up to 50 thumbs-up are counted)	1 per "thumbs-up"
Receive a violation	-10

Level	Points	Questions	Answers	Comments	Follows	Ratings
7	25000+	20	160	40	100	unlimited
6	10000-24999	20	160	40	100	unlimited
5	5000-9999	20	160	40	100	unlimited
4	2500-4999	20	160	40	100	unlimited
3	1000-2499	15	120	20	100	unlimited
2	250-999	10	80	20	100	unlimited
1	1-249	5	20	10	100	unlimited

*All limitations are per day

Quora

Quora is another great site to receive answers for your queries. They don't have a feature like Yahoo to choose the best answer, but Quora members can upvote the most helpful answer.

Thus, answers that provide the best value will be displayed on top, which will get more visibility.

You can post images and links along with your answer. Here's a screenshot of a typical Quora Q & A.

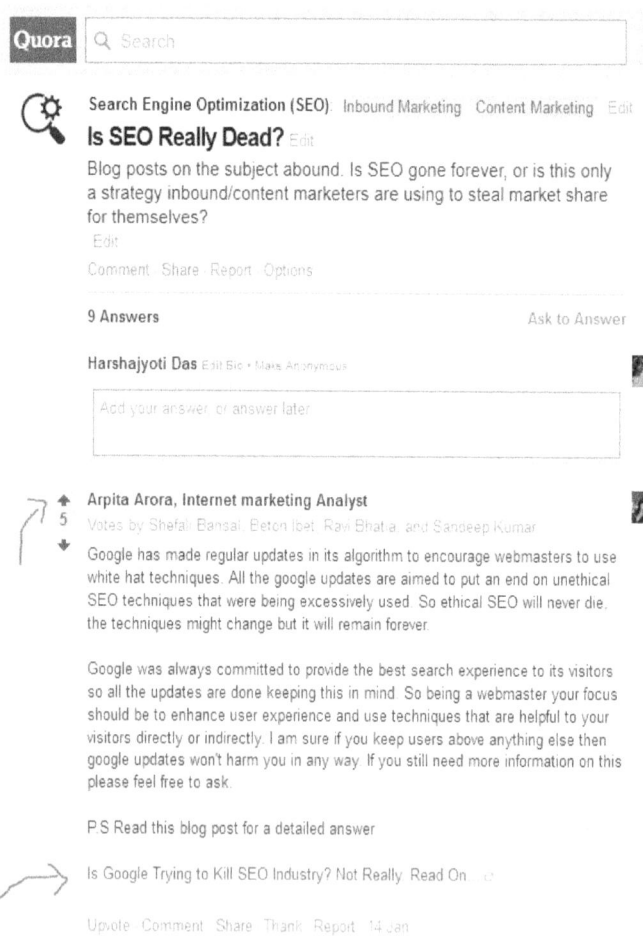

Apart from the usual questions and answers, Quora also has a section where you can post your own articles. It's like having a blog on a big platform that can easily reach thousands of users on Quora.

1) *Roopkund Lake – The Mysterious lake of Skeleton.*

Roopkund Lake ... (more)

The 'write post' feature on Quora will work similar to posting an article on Hubpages or Squidoo. If you create a community (build followers), then you can get your post in front of a wide audience. Whether it's your blog or off-site marketing, you will need to work on building your audience. It might seem like building an audience on each platform (Twitter, Facebook, Quora, Tumblr, Triberr, etc.) is very cumbersome, but once it's done, it will act as a source of free traffic.

How to Monitor New Questions on These Sites?

You have two options. Either log in to those sites and find the questions manually, or automate the process, using a software like BuzzBundle *(I am **NOT** affiliated to them)*.

BuzzBundle is a software that will semi-automate posting on Q & A sites, social media sites, forums and blogs.

Here are a few salient features of BuzzBundle:

1. You can create unlimited profiles for different websites

2. Use proxies
3. Monitor multiple (up to 10) projects per campaign
4. Create new social profiles from within the software
5. Comment on blogs and forums directly
6. Retweet, reply, and send private messages on Twitter
7. Find links to your site from blogs, forums and social media sites
8. Find who's linking back to your site already
9. Track your competitors
10. You can easily switch between multiple accounts

Footprints to Find More Q And A Sites

There are a lot of Q and A forums that you can scrape by searching for specific search terms in Google. Here are a few footprints that you can directly copy and paste on Google to find question and answer sites.

If you want to find a niche specific site, then add the keyword as a suffix.

E.g.: *"Powered by Question2Answer" keyword*

Here are a few popular Q & A platforms. The footprints are as follows:

*"**Data Modelers QA** is a community service provided by Datanamic"*

*"**Powered by Question2Answer"**

- "Powered by Question2Answer" +"asked * ago by" -site:question2answer.org +"KW"
- *"Snow Theme by Q2A Market"*
- *"Theme Designed By: Pixel n Grain"*
- *"To see more, click for the full list of questions or popular tags."*
- *"Recent questions and answers" Question2Answer*
- *"Designed by Axiologic SaaS" Question2Answer*

*"**powered by ASKBOT"**

1. *"Search tip: add tags and a query to focus your search"*
2. *"Content on this site is licensed under a Creative Commons Attribution Share Alike 3.0 license." askbot*

3. *"Hi, there! Please sign in" askbot*

"Powered by Qhub.com"

- *"Answer Questions or Ask a Question"*
- *"Ask a question Provide Feedback"*
- *"Badges Explained" "Asked a question"*

"Powered by OSQA"

- *"questions tags users badges unanswered" "ask a question"*
- +"powered by OSQA" +site:*/questions/ +"KW"
- *"You are welcome to start submitting your question anonymously."*

"Powered by Shapado"

- *"All Shapado.com content and data are available under the Creative Commons Attribution 3.0 license"*

BONUS FOOTPRINTS (not so popular platforms)

- "powered by Answerbase"

- +"powered by Answerbase" +"KW"
- "©2012 Answers All right reserved"+"by WP-Answers." -site:wp-answers.com +intitle:"KW"
- "Powered by Qwench"
- "Question Answer Script"
- "Instant Q&A" "Question & Answers Wordpress Plugin by WP-Answers"
- "Question & Answers WordPress Plugin" "by WP-Answers"
- "Powered by Agriya.com"
- "Anova does not evaluate or guarantee the accuracy of any Anova content"
- "Powered By AlstraSoft AskMe Pro"
- "ExactAsking.com"
- "All images are property of ExactAsking.com and Exact, Inc"
- "©2010 ExactAsking.com"
- "Powered by Askbot version 0.7.43"
- "Powered by Askbot
- "Answer Question script | Powered by AnswerQuestionScript.com"
- "Answer Question Script
- "Powered by AnswerQustionScript.com"
- "Powered by LampCMS"
- "Famous Questions CMS v1.01"
- "by FamousWhy"
- "Famous Questions CMS v1.01 by FamousWhy"
- "Famous Questions CMS"
- "powered by cahoots2"

- "concentrated technology"
- "powered by solace"

I still recommend that you use an online scraper instead of doing it manually. It will save you tons of time. I use scrapebox, but if you want free software, then there's software called, Simple SERP Scraper.

(Non-affiliate Link):
http://www.targetlocal.co.uk/tools/simple-serp-scraper/

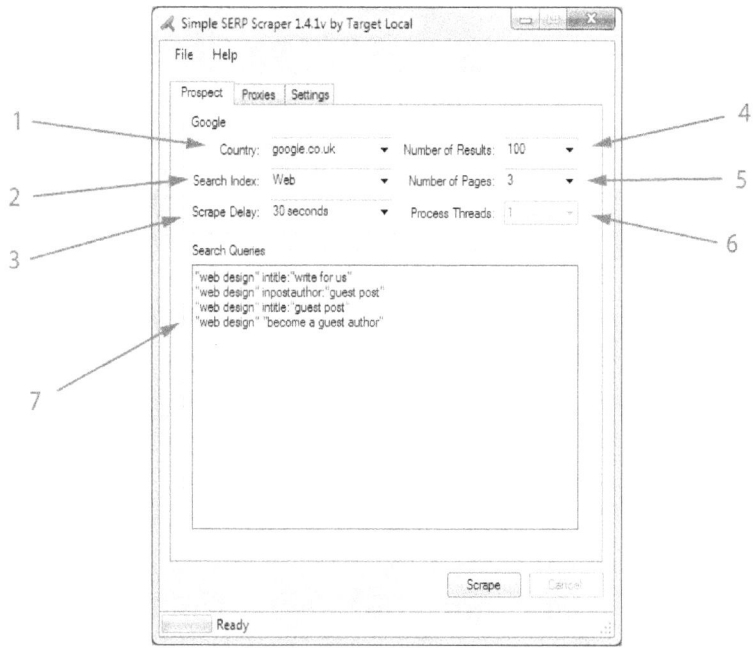

Hiring a Dedicated VA for This Job

Instead of doing the job manually, you can hire a VA (virtual assistant) to do the job for you. Here are some sites via which you can hire your virtual assistant.

1. **Odesk** – You can either pay per project or pay by the hour. They have a built-in employee monitoring software. You can find an average guy from South-East Asia who can speak English for as low as $3/hr. You will get bidders mainly from India, Bangladesh and the Philippines.

2. **Freelancer.com** – It's similar to Odesk, but in my personal experience, I have found that they lack serious bidders. Most people copied and pasted pitches. Freelancers tend to charge a bit more than Odesk workers (in my personal experience). Still, you can give it a try.

3. **Elance.com** – Elance is a better platform than Odesk or Freelancer.com. There are plenty of serious workers from Europe, the USA, and Asia. Although, it

might be a bit costlier compared to Odesk or Freelancer.com

4. **Microworkers.com** – If you want to hire an army of freelancers instead of one, this is the platform you should go for. People will complete a simple task for as low as $0.10.

It's quite necessary that you specify your work details to your VA before commencing your work. If you don't, it might cause serious problem. Most of the time, they won't understand your needs even if they say they do.

Here's what I do:

I create a video by recording my screen using software like eLecta Live Screen Recorder. I show them step-by-step how the work needs to be done. I ask them to watch the video and hit me up if they have any queries. It helps them to easily understand the work you want them to do. Whenever they have any doubts, they can always watch the video and clear their doubts.

I have also found it to be a great time saver. They no longer buzz me on Skype with silly questions.

Chapter 4

Kindle Books

What will be covered in this chapter?

1. What are Kindle books?
2. How can you drive traffic from a Kindle book?
3. How can it help your brand?
4. How to get Kindle books written ?
5. How to use Free books to send traffic?
6. A source to capture emails and re-target them via email marketing

Amazon is the world's 3rd largest search engine after Google and YouTube. What separates, Amazon users from other search engines is that they have a credit card ready in their hands while they are surfing Amazon. It makes Amazon a far more converting search engine than Google.

What Are Kindle Books?

Amazon has taken ebooks to a whole new level with Kindle. You can read Kindle ebooks on not just Kindle devices but also on PCs, tablets and mobiles if you have the free Kindle app installed.

Reportedly, Amazon sells over a million Kindle e-books every week. Evidently, Amazon has also stated that Kindle ebooks sell 50% more than hardcovers and paperbacks. The number has grown exponentially in the last couple of years.

Kindle books are usually self-published by authors. Amazon pays them up to 70% royalty which is way better than traditional publishing houses (~10%).

The minimum word count for a Kindle book is just 2,500 words. However, ebooks with 10k+ words sell much better than 2,500 word ebooks. Thus, it gives a wonderful window of opportunity for first time authors to publish their books and reach a wide audience.

If you think about it, not just the authors but marketers can use Kindle for their business as well. We will discuss more about it in the subsequent section.

How Can You Drive Traffic From A Kindle Book?

Now that you know that millions of Kindle ebooks are downloaded every week, you need to start thinking of ways to monetize it.

There are two ways:

1. **Publish your own books:** Outsource books and get them written by ghostwriters

2. **Advertise on bestselling books:** Contact bestselling books (based on sales rank) and offer to advertise your logo/banner on their books.

Publishing your own books

Publishing your own book is really easy on Kindle. It takes less than a day to get your book uploaded and published.

When you have your own books, here are a few ways to convert visitors:

Offer something for free - Offer something for free as a gift to your readers for buying your book. You can capture their email addresses during the process. It's an effective lead generation technique.

Build your followers - With the help of your book, you can build your Twitter or Facebook followers. People will follow you on social media if they like reading your book.

On a side note, you can also read my guide on ***Building Twitter Followers***. http://bit.ly/twitter-guide-fireyourmentor

Text hyperlinks - While writing your book, you can hyperlink your text to link back to your website. Do it sparingly, so that it doesn't look like spam.

Whether a person reads your book on a Kindle, tablet, mobile or pc, he can easily surf the internet.

Use product images - You can use product images with a price wisely within your book, so that buyers will have an urge to check out your site.

Use anecdotes about your company/business - People get hooked into a book when they read a story. If that story involves your business or company, people will be more eager to know about you and your business.

I know an author who coaches people to build their Kindle publishing business. He religiously uses anecdotes about his business, his clients, and his staff.

Offer opportunities - When you are in front of a wide audience, you can sell any and everything as long as you are doing it right.

Think of it as speaking to a hundred people in a conference. If you want to convert these people into your customers, what opportunity would you provide them? Discounted coupons, freebies, etc.?

Use 'The Rule of Reciprocation' to send customers to your website. 'The Rule of Reciprocation' states that when you offer something to a person, he gets the urge to give you something in return.

When I say you need to give something to your readers, I am not just pointing towards materialistic items like a free t-shirt, but it can also be the knowledge about something.

Let's say you are a guy who owns a retail shop that sells software. You might want to advise your readers to wait for four months before they buy a new laptop because XYZ company will launch a new product in five months at half the market rate.

When you offer information that people can't resist from appreciating, that's when you can profit from 'The Rule of Reciprocation'.

I apply a simple technique with all my subscribers.

Whenever somebody subscribes to my mailing list, I send them an email immediately asking them to reply me with one of their problems. I try my best to solve it for free.

Here's the exact email I send out:

Hi XYZ,

I want you to email me right now, and tell me what your biggest struggle is at the moment. What are you working towards or trying to change, but having a difficult time with?
Really, hit reply right now and let me know. While I can't reply to everyone, I personally read every single one of these emails.

Regards,
Harsh

People hit me with emails asking me to help them with their blog, and some even talk about their professional problems. I go through as many queries as I can and reply to the best of my knowledge. It creates an instant connection. So, the next time I go up to them for help, it will be hard for them to deny it.

How Can It Help Your Brand?

Being a published author can directly impact your brand reputation. The designation, 'author' shouts out loud that a person is knowledgeable in his field and can be trusted.

Every time you send an email to your list, instead of referring to yourself as just the CEO or Founder (which is a common designation); you can also write 'Author'.

You can put an image of your bestselling book on your site. It is also an unique selling proposition when it comes to brand value. It will separate you from your competitors. Customers are more likely to trust an author who has written a book in his industry than some random seller.

The same designation can help you get links

Being a book author has many perks. One of them is the invitations to get interviewed. Whether it's a podcast, video interview or a written interview, you will be able to leave a link back to your website. Also, imagine the amount of referral traffic you can get from these interviews. Most of them will go viral on YouTube or iTunes.

You can also approach blog owners and ask them to interview you on their blog. Interestingly, people are more open to doing interviews than accepting a guest post. Hence, it's an easier approach to get links and referral traffic.

PS: The email format to pitch for interviews is mentioned after a few pages.

There are a lot of sites where you can add your books. They were created with the idea of helping indie authors.

Some of them allow you to add a link back to your site. An example of one of them is http://bookgoodies.com/. They will not only help you promote your book but will also help with your reputation management.

Negative feedback is inevitable, and when negative press (such as RipOffReports) shows up on Google, it affects you brand reputation. People end up spending thousands of dollars to get their name cleared.

You can easily avoid it by taking some simple measures. One of them is to add the brand name alongside your book when you submit it to those sites.

So, the next time when people search for your brand name, these sites will show up on search engines, including Google. They will not only promote you as an author, but will also prevent negative press from showing up on the front page of Google.

Here's a list of over 78 sites where you can submit your book:

http://pixelscroll.com/feature-your-product/

http://ebookshabit.com/for-authors/

http://www.centsibleereads.com/p/for-authors.html

http://bookpromocentral.com/submit-to-bpc-2/

http://bargainebookhunter.com/feature-your-book/

http://thefrugalereader.com/promotional-opportunities/

http://www.indiesunlimited.com/submissions/

http://yapromocentral.com/submit-to-yapc/

http://www.booktweetingservice.com/

http://blog.orangeberrypromo.com/2012/09/orangeberry-free-me/

http://www.theereadercafe.com/p/authors.html

http://freedigitalreads.com/author-submissions/

http://kindlebookpromos.luckycinda.com/?page_id=283

http://authormarketingclub.com/

http://www.freebooksy.com/editorial-submissions

http://www.kindle-freebies.com/about.html

http://www.iauthor.uk.com/ads/advertise?Itemid=106

http://askdavid.com/free-book-promotion

http://kindlebookpromos.luckycinda.com/?page_id=283

http://www.facebook.com/freeebookdeal

http://www.kindleboards.com/ads/

http://www.thekindlebookreview.net/advertise-here/

http://www.freebookshub.com/authors/

http://trindiebooks.com/category/book-of-the-day/

http://thefrugalereader.com/submissions/

http://digitalbooktoday.com/12-top-100-submit-your-free-book-to-be-included-on-this-list/

http://www.dailyfreebooks.com/promote-your-kindle-book.html

http://bookdealsdaily.wordpress.com/

http://indiehousebooks.com/authors-corner/

http://awesomegang.com/submit-your-book/

http://www.bookblast.co/advertise.shtml

http://bookgoodieskids.com/submit-your-free-book-days/

http://thekindleromancereview.blogspot.co.uk/p/advertise-with-us.html

http://blog.orangeberrypromo.com/sign-up-sponsorship-2/

http://indaindex.com/

http://flurriesofwords.blogspot.co.uk/p/book-advertising.html

http://www.mybookandmycoffee.com/p/free-ebook-feature.html

http://bookgoodies.com/submit-your-free-kindle-days/

http://www.bookslut.com/advertise/rates.php

http://addictedtoebooks.com/node/add/ebook

http://www.ereaderiq.com/contact/

http://www.bookbub.com/

http://www.goodreads.com/advertisers

http://www.fkbooksandtips.com/for-authors/

http://fireapps.blogspot.co.uk/p/app-developers-authors.html

http://www.kindlemojo.com/contact-info/

http://the-cheap.net/authors/

http://bookgoodies.com/submit-your-free-kindle-days/highlight-your-free-kindle-days/

http://kindlebookpromos.luckycinda.com/?page_id=363

http://addictedtoebooks.com/free

http://www.snickslist.com/

http://www.kindleboards.com/index.php/topic,97167.0.html

http://ereadernewstoday.com/category/free-kindle-books/

http://bookgoodies.com/get-featured/

http://freekindlefiction.blogspot.co.uk/p/tell-us-about-free-books.html

http://kindlebookpromos.luckycinda.com/?page_id=363

http://digitalbooktoday.com/join-our-team/

http://www.frugal-freebies.com/p/submit-freebie.html

http://www.free-ebooks.net/submissionForm.php

http://www.indiebookpromo.com/submit-to-ibp-3/

http://www.freebookdude.com/p/list-your-free-book.html

http://www.justkindlebooks.com/submit-your-book/

https://docs.google.com/spreadsheet/viewform?formkey=dHI3UVVZdTZkWU03d2w3aDExbXk5MEE6MQ#gid=0

http://ebookshabit.com/book-of-the-day-contact-form/

http://freekindlefiction.blogspot.co.uk/p/guaranteed-post.html

http://ebookimpresario.com/advertise/

http://www.thatbookplace.com/free-promo-submissions/

http://www.pixelofink.com/sfkb/

http://indie.kindlenationdaily.com/?page_id=705

http://www.independentauthornetwork.com/join-ian.html

http://www.goodkindles.net/p/submit-your-book.html

http://indie.kindlenationdaily.com/?page_id=642

http://www.bookdaily.com/authorsignup

http://www.efictionfinds.com

http://www.kindleboards.com/free-book-promo

http://www.bookbrowse.com/information/index.cfm?fuseaction=advertisers

http://ebookdailydeals.com/contact.cfm

Makes Guest Posting Simpler:

People get bombarded with guest posting requests every day from unknown people. It's obvious that most people would simply ignore all of them, unless they see a reason not to.

In my own personal experience, when I pitch a guest posting topic to a blog owner, 90% of them will never reply. The 'reply rate' increased by almost 200% after I started pitching as a published author.

When you introduce yourself as an author, it increases your chance of getting your guest article published on a 3rd party blog by a huge margin.

Here's the exact email that I send:

Hey XYZ,

*I am looking for interview & guest blogging opportunities on your blog. I will also share it with my audience. You can expect over **50+ social shares** from them, which **will give your site a little more exposure**.*

I am the author of a bestselling book on 'Conversion Optimization' (http://www.amazon.com/dp/B00J4TR7W2/ *). I blog at* http://FireYourMentor.com *.*

If you are interested, you can email me a couple of questions for the written interview. If you want me to write a guest blog, do let me know if you have any particular topic/idea in mind.

Some of my past interviews:

- http://www.bloggersideas.com/interview-with-harshajyoti-das-founder-of-fireyourmentor/
- http://www.dailymorningcoffee.com/the-naked-truth-about-harshajyoti-das/
- http://www.treptalks.com/guest-interviews/trep-talks-interview-harshajyoti-das-fireyourmentor-com/

Thank You!

Regards,
Harshajyoti Das

Co-Founder and CEO at http://Munmi.org
Facebook:
https://www.facebook.com/TheHarshajyotiDas
Twitter: @jr_sci

Help To Get Press via HARO (HelpAReporterOut.com)

HARO is a platform via which reporters and journalists can interview sources for their stories. It gives a great opportunity to sources to feature their names in both print and digital media.

If you sign up as a source, you will receive 3 emails a day, each containing around 10-20 opportunities. You will need to pitch immediately, as thousands of other sources will receive the same email.

Here's what a HARO query looks like:

2) Summary: Stocks and highway construction

Name: George Yacik Consumers Digest

Category: Business and Finance

Email: query-3x4d@helpareporter.net

Media Outlet: Consumers Digest

Deadline: 7:00 PM EST - 14 May

Query:

President Obama has proposed spending $302 billion over four years on transportation projects, primarily highways. Which publicly-traded companies stand to benefit the most from that, and why?

Requirements:

Stock market analysts and financial advisers. Emailed responses are greatly appreciated.

Back to Top Back to Category Index

People who seek media opportunities can monitor these queries (or hire a VA to do the job). They can then pitch and contribute to those queries, where they are qualified.

Usually, the pitch requirements are mentioned in the query. Reporters want an expert opinion. Being an author, they will trust you more than your competitors, who are trying to get featured in the same media.

Hence, being an author will add to your advantage.

What are the things that you need to remember while pitching?

Keep your pitch short and to the point. Don't brag about yourself or your achievements. Just mention it in the signature.

Here's an example of an ideal pitch:

New Pitch - Strategies for Managing Time in Daily Life: Hi
Lindsay,
I'm responding to your HARO query about managing time
in daily life.

Favorite Source

My strategies:
I am a big fan of to-do lists. They seem simple (and maybe even
compulsive!) but having an idea of what needs to get done is extremely
helpful for me.

Within my to-do lists another strategy of mine is that I denote what must
get done and what would be nice to have. This helps me prioritize in
case what I need to accomplish gets too lengthy.

My to-do lists span work and my personal life and I have another simple
strategy that helps me stay organized within both. I use a daily planner
(an old fashioned, bound one) which includes my personal life items written
directly in it. I include work items as well but I write those
post-its which I place on top of the day in the planner. This
way everything is kept organized but with some separation.

I know studies suggest that striking off a line item from a to-do
list gives the sense of progress and accomplishment; being able to rip off
a post-it and throw it into the garbage is even more fulfilling!

About me:
Marketing Manager and Culture Team Lead at a website; personal brander,
blogger, and aspiring coach living in Atlanta, GA.

My blog with more info and picture: janeonchange.blogspot.com/

Please let me know of any questions, thanks so much!

Jane

Sites similar to HARO:

- http://www.pressking.com/

- http://www.sourcebottle.com.au/

- http://reporterconnection.com/

How to Get Kindle Books Written? (Size, Outsource, Work Count, Design, Editing, Format)

Since you know the advantages of getting your book published, let's discuss how you can get them written, edited and formatted.

How big should your book be?

A Kindle book can be as small as an 8 page booklet with just 2500 words. I wouldn't advise you to write small.

The sole reason for you to write a book is to show yourself as an authority so that people can trust you. You certainly wouldn't want to ruin that. I would vote for a big fat book that has at least 15,000 words.

After publishing 7-8 books (under different pen names), I can say that a book sells much better if it has more than 10,000 words.

How Do You Outsource Your Book?

You can find any freelance writer to do your work. The only thing you need to remember is that you should provide specific instructions and look over the entire work.

The hiring process is always challenging. You will find numerous requests from incompetent people claiming to be experts. It becomes extremely difficult to select a person among a bunch of idiots. If you are in the hiring process already, you will understand what I am referring to.

Hence, I always provide a trial project to test their skills. Once I shortlist the candidates, I get on Skype with them and talk to them face-to-face. It helps me to decide and hire based on not just skills but also character.

There are numerous places where you can find a freelancer. Elance, Freelancer, Odesk, and Fiverr, to name a few. Most non-native writers will charge anywhere between $2-$5 for a 500 words article. If they quote you more, dump them. You will find cheap writers if you keep searching.

Hence, to write a 10,000 word eBook, it will cost you anywhere between $40-$100.

Asking Them to Do Proper Research

When you want to get a book written, you don't want your writers to simply re-write articles from the internet. The book should have something new, something informative, that can help your readers.

On top of that, they should add anecdotes to make the book more appealing.

Provide them chapter ideas along with subtitles

If you want to personalize your book with your own ideas, then you need to provide these ideas to your writers. Make a long list of all your ideas as bullets in a doc file. Also, categorize them as chapter ideas and paragraph ideas.

Get ideas from YouTube

YouTube is more like an online university with thousands of courses. Ask your readers to watch YouTube videos by well-known speakers on your topic. They are required to take notes using a pen and a paper just like they do in a class.

Once they have sufficient ideas about that topic, they can start writing the book in their own language.

Ideas from Slideshares

There are thousands of Slideshare presentations on any topic you want to find. Your writers can also take ideas from these Slideshare presentations.

The reason why I like Slideshares is because the information is concise and is laid down in points. It's quite easy to find your own sub-topic ideas.

Moreover, there's less scope of re-writing the exact content of somebody else's work. Your writers will be able to write in their own language and turn those couple of points into a whole book.

How to Use Free Books to Send Traffic

If you are not interested in the royalty but only traffic from these ebooks, then you should either give them away for free or price them at 99 cents.

I hope you are already aware of the royalty percentage by Amazon. If I haven't made it clear, let me do it now.

$0.99 - $2.98 - 30% Royalty
$2.99 - $9.99 - 70% Royalty

So, it's always a wise idea to price your book where it earns 70% royalty. If you price your book below $2.99, your sales are likely to increase.

Hence, make a decision before pricing your book. Do you want to get more sales or more royalties?

The price-match technique:

Free books get huge number of downloads every day. Think 100+!

If you want to give away your book for free on Amazon, you cannot do it right away. You will need use the price match technique.

Here's how to do it:

1. List your Amazon book at $2.99

2. List your book on smashwords.com for free

Then notify Amazon, using this link, that the book is available for free on Smashwords. They will match the price and will make your book available for free.

Let me give you an idea of how good a free book can sell. My books are enrolled under "KDP select," which gives me the option to run a promo for 5 days when my book's available for free.

Here's a screenshot of my sales for 1 book that went free for 3 days:

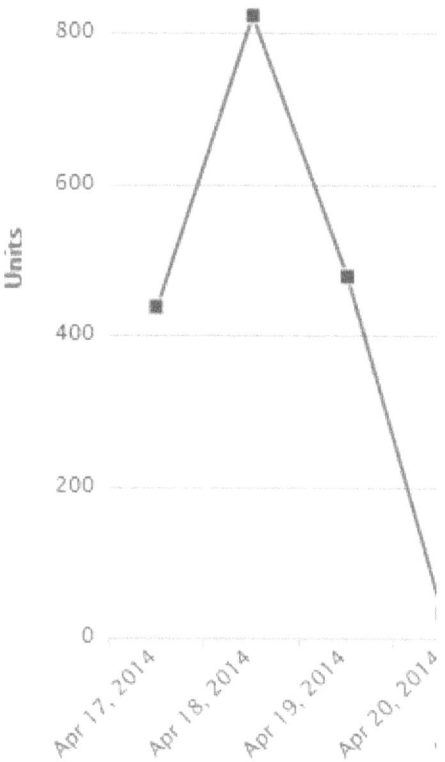

The book sold **448** copies on day 1, **821** copies on day 2 and **463** copies on day 3. A total of **1732 copies** downloaded within 3 days!

A Source To Capture Emails and Re-Target Them via Email Marketing

Email marketing has been by far the best approach for any marketer since the beginning of ecommerce.

Your Kindle book will act as a source to capture email leads. The concept is simple. Offer your readers something for free that's worth something to them.

If you offer another free eBook on the same or similar topic, the reader is most likely to convert. Similarly, you can offer a free report or free consultation.

With your website, you try to capture leads via pop ups and opt in forms. With Kindle, it's somewhat similar.

The leads from Kindle are more valuable. Here's why. Leads that you gain from Amazon Kindle are online spenders. They are unlike the leads from your website, who are mostly in the surfing mode.

Once you have the emails, re-target them via email marketing. I bet these leads will convert better (in terms of sales) than the leads generated via your website.

I have previously posted my email template that I use to make an instant connection with my readers. Use the same one in this case.

Chapter 5

Email Marketing

While writing this book, I have written for both veterans and newbies. To be honest, this book will be mostly read by small business owners who are tired of spending on SEO and getting penalized time and again.

Hence, here's a chapter on email marketing. We all know that you need to capture leads and then email them with offers, but is that enough? How are you doing it differently than millions of other marketers who are targeting the same consumers?

In order to say, "NO SEO FOREVER", you need to reach to a point where you have a loyal subscriber list and you can make a living from them. That's the goal.

Things we will cover in this chapter:

1. The concept of email marketing
2. Different email marketing software in the market and their comparison

3. Tips to capture leads within a website (with images)
4. Tips to capture leads from Facebook (with images) http://blog.getresponse.com/understanding-target-audience-landing-pages.html
5. Tips to capture leads from Kindle books (with images)
6. Examples of great email templates http://www.quicksprout.com/2012/12/07/the-link-builders-guide-to-email-outreach/
7. A few amazing email marketing examples by industry leaders http://blog.hubspot.com/marketing/email-marketing-examples-list
8. Link request email templates to blog owners (not just for links but also for referral traffic)

The Concept of Email Marketing

Everybody checks emails daily, and sometimes 4-5 times a day. It's a direct way to reach your prospective customers. It works even better when you re-target people who have subscribed via your website.

An email works hundred times better than a tweet or a like on FB. <1% will see your tweet on Twitter and <20% will see your update on Facebook. On the other hand, email open rate is usually more than 50%.

Earlier, people could email anybody they wanted with marketing emails. But now, spam is a serious issue. As per the **Can Spam Act** by the FTC (Federal Trade Commission), you are not allowed to email any random person with a commercial email without their permission. You can only do so if you have their permission.

Different Email Marketing Software in the Market and Their Comparison

We will talk briefly about 3 leading email marketing softwares:

1. Aweber
2. Get Response
3. Mailchimp

Aweber

Aweber is the email marketing software most commonly used by professionals. It's a bit costlier than Get Response and Mailchimp, but it has more features than its counterparts.

I use Aweber and I love it. It will cost you $19.95/month.

You have the ability to quickly create opt-in forms that can be placed on any site using Javascript or HTML code. If you are a business owner without any programming skills, then Aweber is an easy choice to make.

Their inbox rate is much better than Get Response or Mailchimp.

That being said, the only drawback I have seen on Aweber is that they lack a responsive design for emails and opt-in forms.
Aweber goes a step further to ensure a spam-free experience for users. You cannot upload an email list directly to Aweber. You need to ask permission from your list once again before adding on Aweber.

Aweber insists that you use a double-opt in for your customers. It helps them to keep spam complains at bay. Your account is most likely to be free from spam traps (not actual emails) as well.

Get Response

Get Response has all the features of Aweber, and the pricing is almost similar.

Here's how Get Response differs from Aweber:

1. They have a responsive design for emails and opt-in forms.
2. You can easily import emails from a CSV/Excel file

Downsides:

The delivery rate is a bit lower than Aweber. Since you can import unknown emails from a CSV file, there's a chance that some people may abuse the system. Hence, it affects the reputation of the whole company.

Mailchimp:

If you are looking at email marketing software that you can use for free or nominal cost, Mailchimp is your answer.

They have a free plan that allows up to 2000 email subscribers. You can easily import emails from a CSV/Excel file.

The downside is that they are less reliable than Aweber and Get Response. They are strict on sending marketing emails with a dubious link.

I have had a free account with them for 4 years now (with less than 1000 subscribers) but to date I haven't found their opt-in forms. I still doubt if they have any. If they have a feature for opt-in forms, it really hard to locate.

I do like their reporting better than Aweber.

Unless and until you have $10 to invest every month on email marketing software, opt for Mailchimp. Otherwise else, skip it and sign up with Aweber or Get Response.

I would like to add that if you plan to transfer email subscribers from Mailchimp to Aweber, you will need to ask their permission once again. It's obvious that you will lose 80% of your subscribers in the process.

So, make a wise decision. Alternatively, if you want to import them to Get Response in the future, you can easily do it without asking for their permission once again.

Tips to Capture Leads from Within a Website

If you don't have a system to catch leads on your website, then you are probably doing the biggest mistake in ecommerce.

When you get visitors to your website via Google or social media sites, you lose them forever if you don't capture their emails. They are probably never going to visit your site again. If you get 100 visitors a day on your website, you lose 36,500 visitors every year.

On average you should get at least 1% conversion rate if you do your homework properly. That's 365 visitors in a year at the lowest.

Each lead is worth around $10-$20 in most cases. On average you are losing $3650-$7300. If your website receives 500 visitors every day, you can lose up to $36,500 in a year.

I am just giving you an idea on what you are losing if you haven't been capturing emails from your website yet.

If you are someone who has been capturing emails but haven't run a profitable email marketing campaign, then you are doing something wrong. The reason behind that can be not being able to create a trusted relationship, not interacting enough, sounding too sales oriented, or not offering a genuine product for their needs.

Unconventional Pop-ups that convert:

Pop ups are the best way to capture website visitors. There are three kinds of pop-ups:

1. Entry pop up
2. Exit pop up
3. Pop up with a timer

Entry pop-up:

The pop-up that you see when you enter a website is called an entry pop-pop. I am not a big fan of entry pop ups. They do convert when you put a pop up with an exciting offer right in the face of a customer, but I wouldn't recommend you to use it.

Here are the reasons why:

1. Why would someone give their email ID on their first visit? They don't even know you.

2. It increases the site bounce rate. Most people will close the browser when they see a pop up.

There are industry leaders like Neil Patel who use entry pop ups and it converts well for them.

The reason for that is that people already know him. Brands like Coca Cola, Pepsi, and KFC can all use an entry pop up, but when somebody who doesn't have a worldwide known brand uses entry pop up, it acts negatively.

Exit Pop Up:

Exit pop ups are a new kind of pop up that tracks the mouse cursor. Whenever a person tries to leave the page, an exit pop up shows up.

It enhances the user experience. A person is more likely to respond to a pop-up when he is finished reading an article rather than while he is in the middle of it.

Here's a screenshot of an exit pop up at www.healcancer.org. If you happen to visit the site, please stop by and say hi to Cindy in the comments.

Pop Up With a Timer

A pop up with a timer is a pop up that you can schedule to show up after 'n' seconds. If you time it at 10 seconds, the pop-up will appear only after 10 seconds of someone browsing through your site.

If you need a free pop up, I recommend using http://sumome.com/. I have come across this plugin lately. It's a wonderful free plugin with all the functionalities of a paid one.

Opt-in forms on the sidebar and after the post

Another way to capture emails is to install opt-in forms on the sidebar. Matthew Woodward of http://www.matthewwoodward.co.uk/ does this brilliantly. **Here's a screenshot:**

How I Built A Top 100 Blog In 12 Months & How You Can Do It Too!

On 19 08 13 In Tutorials, by Matthew Woodward

This is the story of how this blog became a Technorati Top 100 Business Blog in just 1 year. I even took a month off! Join me on my journey and I will share everything I did with you step by step over my shoulder. I have managed to achieve quite a lot with the [...]

473 Comments   Leave Your Response

[UPDATE2] Why Your Webhost Cannot Be Trusted – How WP Engine Hijacked My Business

On 29 08 14 In Reviews, by Matthew Woodward

When I first moved my hosting over to WP Engine I was highly impressed. They were very helpful, support took ownership of problems and site speed was incredible. As someone that has been in the game as long as I have it is rare to find a hosting company that provided the level of support [...]

Welcome To My Blog!
Let me introduce myself, my name is...

Matt

No no, Matt Cutts, but I am better at SEO than him. P. I make a great living online with SEO and I will teach you how you can as well.

You Can Find Me On...

Get My Latest Posts

Sign up for my newsletter to get the latest blog updates direct to your inbox

Your Name

Your Email

Subscribe Now

WARNING! I **do not** send ANY 'Guru' spam or affiliate promotions

Sponsors

Lewis Ogden, the guy behind http://www.cloudincome.com, has a personalized opt-in form below every article. He also has a thumbnail of his picture that builds credibility and conversion.

Using a Top 'Hello' Bar:

The orange horizontal bar you see on top of a website is called a "hello bar". It was originally designed by hellobar.com, but now there are many versions, like the one from ViperChill (as you see on FireYourMentor.com).

They are clean and have proven to be instrumental in increasing conversions by a huge margin. You can either promote an offer or use it as an opt-in form. Try it out on your own site and compare the clicks with other opt-ins. It should be comparatively higher.

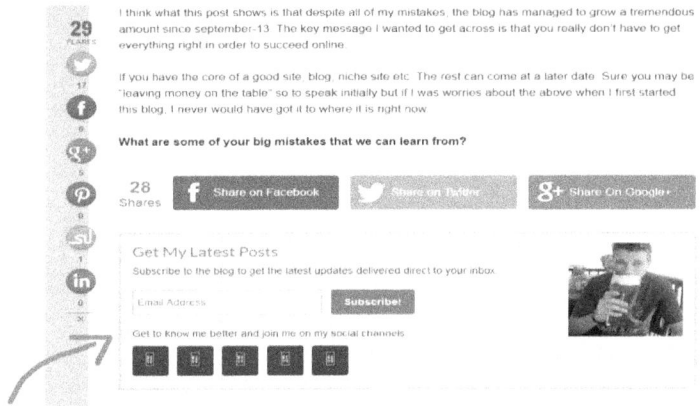

Footer Slide out Opt-In Form:

You can also place your opt-in form near the end of the page. There are two ways to do it. One is to install a slide-up horizontal footer bar (just like the top hello bar), and the second is to install a square slide up on either the left or right footer.

It only shows up when a visitor scrolls all the way down to the footer of your site. It means your visitor is already engaged with your content.

Here's a screenshot to make it clearer:

Horizontal footer slide-up

You can use the 'Aweber footer slideup' plugin for WordPress. If you don't have an account with Aweber, there are other alternatives.

You can also use "**End Page Slide Box** plugin" along with **"Wp-Insert** plugin" to install the opt-in form in the footer of your site that slides up.

Tips to Capture Leads from Facebook

Facebook is the largest social media network out there. You can harness the power by capturing leads from Facebook. In this section, I will discuss in brief the whole idea. In the next Volume, we will cover the entire subject and discuss it in detail.

Alright, so you do know about Facebook Ads right?

Here's the whole idea:

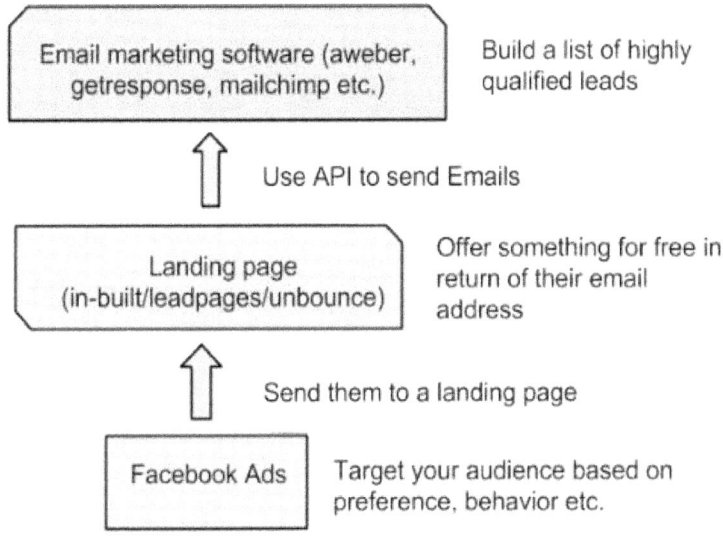

Once you set up your Facebook ads, send them to a landing page where you can capture their email IDs in exchange for a free report or something similar.

Once you have the emails in your email marketing software, schedule an auto responder. You need to build a new relationship with your newly collected leads.

In the next volume, we will learn how you can harness the power of social media to drive traffic to your site. Let's take another step towards "NO SEO FOREVER" with it.

Chapter 6

Build an Asian Sales Army

This gets interesting. We will combine the power of traditional marketing with modern technology.

Asia has the cheapest labor in the world. If you were to hire an assistant in the US or UK, it will cost you at least $2000 every month. You could get the same from Asian countries like India, Bangladesh, China, the Philippines, Pakistan, or Vietnam for $200/month. If you hire them part time, it will cost you less than $100/month.

Now, I understand that you can't outsource any and everything. You need skilled labor. If you have a marketing strategy, you can easily outsource them those repetitive jobs that don't need many skills.

Imagine your competitor has 50 full time employees in their online sales team. If you go out there and hire 500 part time employees, don't you think you will have an unfair advantage over them?

Don't think it's impossible. It's actually simpler than it sounds.
The other day, I was searching for a good air conditioner when I came across this idea.

Let me give you an example and show you how you can harness the power of an Asian Sales Army.

Let's say you have teamed up with a Chinese manufacturer to create your own brand of smartphone (think alibaba.com).

For market penetration, you have already reduced the price. What else can you do? **Get the word out in public.**

If people have never heard about your brand, they will never buy your phones. Thanks to the internet, people do their research before buying anything. Exploit the same.

First, create a list of all your competitors - Apple, Samsung, Nokia, Motorola, etc.

Second, create an Excel spreadsheet of all the possible mobile phones (brands and series).

Third, add another column to the Excel sheet named as "suffix". A suffix is what a person would add after a phone name to search on Google.

Example: *iPhone battery life.* Here, 'battery life' is a suffix.

Examples of a few suffixes are:

1. any good
2. battery life
3. price
4. dealer in {city name}
5. reviews
6. problems
7. complaints
8. or {other brand name}
9. vs {other brand name}
10. won't turn on
11. hangs frequently

You can go on and on. There will be hundreds of different suffixes you can come up with.

Once you have a few hundred suffixes in your list, you can combine them with the brand & product names.

BINGO!! You have a list of over a thousand keywords people use to search Google before making their purchasing decision.

Now go ahead and hire a couple of VAs. I have already talked about the different platforms to hire freelancers and virtual assistants.

You can either hire a couple of freelancers from Odesk or Elance or post a job on microworkers.com.

Let's talk about what kind of job you can allot to a guy you just hired from Odesk.com.

Pay him by the hour. Usually, it will cost you less than $2/hr. Check his English skills before hiring him. You will need them if he is going to spread the word about your company.

First, send him the list of your competing brands and the suffixes you have just generated. You will need to do the initial hard work, since you will know your industry better than anyone else. Of course, you can also ask your staff to generate the Excel sheets instead.

Tell your VA to search Google/Yahoo/Bing and find discussion boards, forums, and review sites that show up on the first page for each keyword.

Ask him to go on each site and register a brand new account. His account should be like that of a consumer who has recently purchased your product. He will take part in these discussions and promote your brand.

Let's say someone has posted a query on Yahoo Answers:

Q: Which is better? Samsung Galaxy S2 or iPhone 4?

There will already be a lot of replies from other people. Your guy can get in the middle and say something like:

"I have both iPhone and {your-brand-name}. IPhone is better, but if you were to compare it with an Android phone, then I would have to suggest {your-brand-name}. I have used {your-brand-name}, which is 50% cheaper than Samsung Galaxy S2, but it has more features, better battery, and comes with Android Kit Kat OS. http://link-to-your-site.com"

His answer is not intended to serve the purpose for this one guy who posted this question. Since this query is already on the first page of Google/Yahoo/Bing, you are looking at thousands of impressions every month. All organic, no bullshit marketing.

If it's a review site, even then he can post a similar answer. First, write a review for your competing product (not necessarily negative - it's better to write positive), then write a few words about your brand and why it's better.

Now, imagine if you hire 10 VAs and distribute to them the work to search over thousands of keywords (from the Excel sheet - competitor's brand + suffix) and post about your brand in each one of them.

You can also ask two guys to post on the same forum. If your first VA introduces your brand name for the first time, ask the second VA to back up his claim by saying something like, "My brother uses {your-brand-name}, and it's been working without a problem for 2 years now. I am planning to buy {your-brand-name/model name}, since it has the same features and it's 50% cheaper than any Android phones on the market. I have seen a lot of new upcoming models when I last visited their website. http://link-to-your-site.com"

If you post a job on microworkers.com, you will have to pay each person for each post they make. They will charge from $0.05--$0.20 per comment. You will have to organize the task, because there will be hundreds of workers who will post about your brand. The last thing you want is all of them to post in the same discussion boards with a couple of one liners. It will then be too obvious for everyone to notice. Ask each person to write at least 50-100 words and distribute their work across multiple keywords.

To make it look more natural, ask each one of them to make 3-4 posts for some different consumer products in the same discussion board/public forum/Q&A site/review site.

Once they are done posting to all the keywords on the first page of Google/Yahoo/Bing, ask them to move to the second page, third page, and so on.

After 2-3 months, ask them to re-visit the first page again, as the SERPs have probably changed by now. Rinse and repeat.

Once the word spreads and you penetrate the market, your consumers will do the rest of your job to spread your brand name. You can then focus on paid advertisements and other traffic sources.

Is it ethical?

It's marketing. You are spreading the word about your product to the public. You aren't making any false claims that would harm anybody. You are merely stating the facts about why people should prefer your brand over others. I would once again ask you to avoid misleading people or making any false claims about your company or product. Give your VAs the necessary information about your company and products before commencing the work.

This is just a simple idea of what an Asian Sales Army can do for your brand. You can also come up with other marketing ideas, like asking them to share and talk about your brand on social media, etc. The possibilities are endless.

With that being said, I think this book has offered you enough information to finally say, "No SEO Forever." In the second volume, I will talk about generating traffic from social media sites.

CONCLUSION

A Note to My Readers

I have almost started writing the chapter on Facebook, but then I realized I should divide this book into 2 Volumes. The second volume will solely deal with traffic from social media.
Social media is so huge that I have so much to say. A separate book will also help readers to find a book who are looking for books on social media.

Moreover, it doesn't change the price at all. Readers who have brought Volume 1 will not have to pay a penny extra for Volume 2. I will price both for $2.99 each. I will also have a combo offer for $3.98.

If you have already brought Volume 1 before the Volume 2 was released, then **I will send you the Volume 2 for FREE** when it's released. I don't want you to feel deceived in any way. I will make sure you get the value for your money.

Do sign up as a fan here:
http://getaccess.me/no-seo-forever

I need to be completely honest and transparent here. I need my readers to trust me. Without you, I don't exist. I have decided to take this step for a marketing advantage as well.

Instead of promoting 1 book, I can now promote 3 books simultaneously, which means I can increase my reach by 300%. I can also run 15 KDP free promo days instead of 5 free days.

I do understand that some of you might have wanted everything in one book, and I do apologize for that. Rest assured, I will do complete justice with the 2nd volume.

Regards,

Harsh